5025   LIBRARY
ANDERSON ELEMENTARY SCHOOL

W9-DFY-982

FOOTBAGGING

LARRY DANE BRIMNER

FOOTBAGGING

FRANKLIN WATTS
NEW YORK | LONDON | TORONTO | SYDNEY
A FIRST BOOK | 1988

All photographs including cover photograph courtesy
of the author except for: The World Footbag Association:
pp. 2, 15, 36, 43, 47, 48, 60.

Library of Congress Cataloging-in-Publication Data

Brimner, Larry Dane.
Footbagging/Larry Dane Brimner.
p.   cm.—(A First book)
Bibliography: p.
Includes index.
Summary: Introduces the various games played with a footbag,
including instructions in basic moves and kicks, tips on strategy,
and a guide to clubs and competitions.
ISBN 0-531-10477-X
1. Footbag—Juvenile literature. (1. Footbag.) I. Title
GV960.F66B74 1988
796.33—dc19   87-16481 CIP AC

Copyright © 1988 by Larry Dane Brimner
All rights reserved
Printed in the United States of America
6 5 4 3 2 1

For
Mom and Dad
with Love

CONTENTS

The author is indebted to
Greg Cortopassi and Bruce Guettich
of the World Footbag Association
for freely offering time and information.

For demonstrating their skills for
typewriter and camera, many thanks to
Jody Badger, Meadow Blough,
River Blough, Alfonso Dominguez,
Chris Donofrio, Jack Harris,
Richie Kientz, Chris Phillips,
Bill Wall, and Mark Wendell.

FOOTBAGGING

CHAPTER ONE

WHAT IS FOOTBAG?

*O*ff to the side of the school-yard, five figures stand in a rough circle. One figure tosses a small, round object to his neighbor, who responds by alternately bouncing the object from his right foot to his left. The object plays back and forth until it is kick-passed to another player in the circle. Round and round it goes; and as the kicks require more skill and effort, the small crowd of onlookers nods with approval or voices disappointment. One player stretches out his foot behind and seemingly picks the object out of the air, sending it sailing back into the circle and to another player. Nods of approval. Later, the object glides to another player who lifts his foot—and misses. Disappointment. But the player, undaunted, picks up the object and hand tosses it to another person in the circle. The game begins again.

The sport is called *footbag*.

Officially, footbag is played with a small, round object. Usually made of handsewn leather, or crocheted, a footbag is about 2 inches (5 cm) in diameter and weighs about one ounce. The filler, which gives a footbag its shape and bounce, can vary from manufacturer to manufacturer, but most are packed with plastic pellets.

Footbag is a footsport. That is, it is played with the feet. The basic object of the sport is to keep the footbag airborne and off the ground using only your lower body. Players believe that if you can touch it with your hands, you can kick it with your feet.

Sometimes footbag is called *Hacky Sack*. Hacky Sack, however, is simply one brand of footbag, just as Kleenex is one brand of tissue. One glance at *Footbag World*, the magazine published by the World Footbag Association (WFA), will verify that there are countless varieties of footbags from which to choose.

The game's advocates continue to grow in number. Several national school assembly agencies, the organizations that plan and schedule assemblies into schools in the United States, rank footbag touring teams as one of the top programs offered. Through them, an estimated two million young people in over five thousand schools have been introduced to footbag games.

But footbag isn't only fun and games. There is a serious side, too. Jay Moldenhauer and the Tric Kix footbag club of Flint, Michigan, hosted the first Michigan State Muscular Dystrophy Kick-a-thon in 1985 and raised six hundred and fifty dollars. Child psychiatrists use footbag as an icebreaker and an esteem builder with troubled patients. And countless professional athletes swear by footbag as a warm-up conditioning tool to assist them in their particular sport.

Footbag is played either alone or in teams. It can be played outside or inside. It's both competitive and coopera-

Champion Rita Buckley successfully demonstrates how important feet are in the sport of footbag.

tive. And it's noncontact. Though skill is required, it is challenging and fun to learn. In fact, footbag is so habit forming that some players apply an often used phrase to describe their sport: Kick the habit!

CHAPTER TWO

FOOTBAG ROOTS

*T*he roots of today's footbag games date back to ancient Eastern cultures, where it is believed that the first kicking game was developed by Chinese Emperor Hwang Ti in 2597 B.C. The sport was called *kemari* and used a hair-filled, leather ball that was oblong in shape. Although considered a sport, kemari was also used by the military for physical training and conditioning. Eye/foot synchronization was practiced in much the same way as the martial arts and stressed concentration, coordination, and control.

Today, versions of this original footbag sport exist in all parts of the world. In Nepal, a kicking game is played that uses a coin with a square hole stamped in the center. Goat hair is pulled through the hole to create a cushion, and the coin is kicked back and forth between players.

The Malaysian countries play a footgame that dates back some thousand years. It is called *sepak takraw.* Played with a takraw ball about 6 inches (15 cm) in diameter and made of woven rattan, the game is played over a 5 foot 1 inch (2 m) net on a 20 foot by 44 foot (6 m x 14 m) court and closely resembles a competitive footbag event called footbag net.

Another footbag relative happens to be the most popular sport in the world: soccer. Except in North America, soccer is called *football*, and it is played in more countries than the United Nations has members. According to the Federation Internationale de Football Association, there are more than forty million amateur and professional soccer players worldwide. As soccer grows even more in popularity, new emphasis is being placed on the development of footskills and there is growing interest in American footbag games, because of their focus on controlled foot movements.

Though some people describe American footbag as "miniature soccer," it is really more. No other sport prohibits the use of the upper body. Further, the size of a footbag makes it more challenging to control than a soccer ball. One soccer player said it all: "If you can control a footbag, soccer's a snap."

Footbag, the American version of these ancient games, began its development in Oregon in 1972, when John Stalberger, an athlete and physical therapist, met up with Mike Marshall. Stalberger, who was looking for an activity that would strengthen an injured knee, spent hours playing at a hobby that Marshall had enjoyed. Using a bean bag, the two kicked and bumped the object in a vain attempt to keep it airborne. Not only was the activity fun, but Stalberger also found it excellent therapy for his knee. Obsessed with their hobby/exercise, they would say, "Let's go hack the sack." You can see how the trade name Hacky Sack originated from their play.

The original footbags used by Stalberger and Marshall evolved over time. Experimenting with different sizes and varying the shapes, their initial disc-like designs were made of old denim and filled with rice or beans. But they soon discovered a problem: organic filler turns to mush after excessive kicking and in wet weather. The pair turned to buttons for the next filler, but found they broke down after a few weeks of heavy kicking. It was back to the drawing board.

Their next model was rounder in shape and made of leather for durability. Instead of a natural filler, the new model was filled with hard plastic discs which didn't break down after prolonged kicking. This design became the prototype for the Hacky Sack footbag, and Marshall and Stalberger applied for a U.S. patent.

Tragedy struck, however, in 1975, when Marshall suffered a heart attack. He didn't live to see his creation flood the United States sports market. But the bond between the men was strong, and Marshall's death provided Stalberger with a stronger conviction to pursue their dream.

He continued making refinements to the footbag. He found that a round footbag provided better kicking and a more consistent angle of flight. He replaced the plastic discs with round plastic pellets for filler and discovered that the new footbag now gave a more dependable, natural reaction while in play.

He also made innovations in the "rules" of the game. By restricting the touching of the footbag to only the feet and knees, and by stressing equal use of both sides of the body to control the footbag, Stalberger realized the game could be used as a physical education and athletic training tool.

Because of its portability, footbag became popular with hikers, backpackers, and other active people, and interest in the sport was enough to accommodate the formation of the National Hacky Sack Footbag Players' Association in 1977. But the interest was geographical, limited primarily to Oregon, Washington, and California. Stalberger next devised the game of footbag net, a truly competitive sport, and tournament growth followed. Footbag was on its way to breaking out of its geographical bounds.

A U.S. patent number was finally granted in 1979 on the

Hacky Sack footbag, and in 1983, Wham-O, Inc., bought the North American manufacturing and distribution rights. The World Footbag Association was also established in 1983 to promote, develop, and monitor the rules of footbag sports, and now it boasts thousands of members in more than twenty-two countries. And there is an effort afoot to have footbag games included in the roster of Olympic sports.

Footbag has come a long way since 2597 B.C.

CHAPTER THREE

GETTING STARTED

Footbag has some distinct advantages over other sports. To begin with, equipment is relatively inexpensive. A good quality footbag can be purchased for between five and ten dollars, depending on where it is purchased and the brand chosen. While some sports require special and costly safety equipment, such as helmets or pads, footbag can be played with very little personal risk and any comfortable clothing will do. It isn't necessary to get a bunch of friends together to begin playing, since footbag may be played individually or in groups. Finally, footbag has the added advantage of being an all-weather, all-location type of activity. In good weather, take your footbag outdoors to practice. During rainy or cold weather, gyms or cleared garages make ideal practice areas. Some players have even been known to practice in family rooms, though caution is urged—a footbag is soft, but not one hundred percent harmless should it glance off your foot in the direction of a priceless piece of crystal.

If you plan on playing any of the footbag sports, a footbag is the basic piece of equipment needed. Since a variety of manufacturers market footbags, it is best to experiment before making a purchase. A couple of practice kicks will tell you if a particular footbag will be easy to manipulate. Better yet, if you have friends who are already footbag enthusiasts, ask their advice. Many players agree that the Sipa Sipa brand footbag is easiest for beginners to place and control. Its pliable quality makes it less apt to glance off the foot at awkward angles. It also has less "bounce," which may assist the beginning player. But in the end, the final choice is yours. If at all possible, experiment with several different brands and choose the one that suits you best. (Note that identical models of footbags made by the same company will vary slightly in their reaction, too.)

Footbag players wear almost every type and style of shoe made while playing footbag. And some don't wear shoes at all! However, professional footbag players and those who take the sport seriously suggest wearing court shoes. Unlike jogging shoes, which have flared soles, court shoes have a flatter surface area for precise kicking.

Some players choose low-topped shoes, while others choose shoes with high tops. But whatever the choice, most players who compete personalize their shoes by wearing thick, colorful laces that match their footbag outfit.

Most players prefer to play in shorts because long pants restrict movement. If long pants are worn, players usually wear leg warmers at the ankle and calf to keep the bottoms of the trousers out of the line of vision. Eye contact with the footbag is critical; if you can't see it, you can't kick it!

Shirts are chosen with the same guidelines. They need to be loose enough to allow movement, but not so loose as to obstruct vision.

Many team members and partners wear shorts and shirts that match. When they begin competing for big purses, they usually choose eye-catching colors, and frequently they have logos silk-screened onto their shirts.

Like any other sport, footbag offers the chance to be "discovered," and most players want a look that stands out from the rest. If you have a special look, it can attract the attention of sponsors who might offer you money to promote a product's name. And recently, several footbag players have hit it big with television commercials.

But unless you're extremely talented, your first experience with footbag won't be an easy or spectacular-looking one. It takes hours and hours of practice to be able to place the footbag with accuracy. Indeed, it takes practice just to get a few consecutive kicks without dropping it! But don't be afraid to miss. Everyone does. And unlike other sports—say white water rafting, for instance—the risks in this game are much less serious. Go ahead. Miss.

In fact, the first footbag stunt you'll likely master is the Footbag Fetch. This is easily accomplished when the footbag ricochets off your foot and rolls under a picnic table or bush or sofa or any other object. Simply chase after the footbag, lean over, grasp it, and return to an upright position.

Mastering footbag takes time, patience, and practice. But control will come. At first, you'll get two consecutive kicks. Then three. Then ten. Then you'll be "shreddin' to the max."

Before you begin practice, however, something else needs to be considered. Footbag involves a lot of postures that will be new to your muscles. For top performance and to decrease the risk of muscle damage, develop a stretching routine. Stretching the muscles before and after exercise prevents cramping and helps maintain flexibility. A post-activity stretch also helps relieve soreness.

Stretching should be done slowly to give the muscles time to warm up (or warm down). At the maximum point of any stretch, hold it for ten to thirty seconds. And breathe naturally. If you are having difficulty breathing while stretching, you're not stretching properly.

Several stretches are beneficial to footbag play. Five are detailed on page 25:

STANDING TOE TOUCH

Cross legs, left over right, and bend forward at the waist until you can touch your toes with your fingers. Hold. Repeat this with the right leg crossed over the left leg.

SINGLE FOOT BALANCE

Balance on one foot. With hands cupped under the other foot, pull it tightly toward the waist. Hold. Then alternate legs.

SIDE EXTENSION

With your right hand on your waist, reach overhead with the left hand and bend to the right (as though trying to touch your right foot with your left hand). Hold. Stretch to the left.

SIDE THRUST

From a standing position, step to the right, flexing the right knee and lowering the torso toward the ground. Rest your arms on the flexed knee to maintain balance. Keep the left leg straight and extended. Hold this position, then repeat in the opposite direction.

LEG-TO-SHOULDER

Facing your partner, bring one leg up to your partner's shoulder (right leg to left shoulder; left leg to right shoulder). To maintain balance, grip your partner's wrists. Hold this position, then alternate legs.

The Footbag Fetch

Before competition, Chris Donofrio and
Bill Wall do the side stretch (above)
and the leg-to-shoulder stretch (opposite).

Once stretching has been completed, you'll be ready to begin practicing. To make the learning process easier, visualize each kick before you attempt it. Then practice, initially, without the footbag. Lift your foot into position and meet it with your hand at the contact point. Try to assume the correct posture, and get the feel of each kick.

Next, drop the footbag by hand and attempt each kick in the correct form. As the footbag pops up, catch it and repeat (or perform the Footbag Fetch and repeat).

For an added dimension of fun, practice with a friend. Have your partner toss the footbag to you, while you attempt to get a kick off the toss. After a few practice attempts, exchange roles so your partner will get some practice, too.

Short periods of practice are preferable to longer ones. Since success comes slowly, a short practice period won't discourage you. And sometimes things are just plain easier if you come back to them refreshed.

CHAPTER FOUR

THE KICKS

*H*ave you ever embarked upon a new sport or game only to find the rules or required skills too complicated to master? You won't find that true with footbag. The rules of each footbag activity are straight-forward and easy to understand. And while the skills take time to master, some degree of proficiency is attainable by almost everyone, regardless of age, sex, or fitness level.

If you're like most people, you'll be so excited about your first footbag that you'll want to begin kicking immediately. And probably, you'll become discouraged when the foot-bag fails to obey your attempts to place it.

Stalberger and Marshall experimented with trial-and-error kicks, but they were developing the sport and there was little previous experience they could look to for guidance. You are luckier. The World Footbag Association and other experi-enced kickers have studied footbag style; from this, they have isolated three major and two minor kicks. All footbag games can be played with these five basic kicks. Once you begin to feel comfortable with a couple of them, you will start linking together your kicks and take on the appearance of a pro.

The three major kicks are the Inside Kick, the Outside Kick, and the Back Kick. The Inside Kick is the most basic of these. Before you can rely on keeping a footbag airborne, the Inside Kick must be mastered.

Which kick you choose to practice first will depend on your own individual talent. Most players, however, begin with the Inside Kick, and get the feel of it before proceeding to the others. If you choose to begin with one of the other kicks, that's okay. Just be sure to develop some expertise with a particular kick before attempting a new one. And don't forget to practice old kicks while adding new ones.

INSIDE KICK

The Inside Kick is used when the footbag drops in front of you and between your shoulders. Start by standing in a relaxed manner with your feet about shoulder-length apart and knees slightly flexed. As you slowly bring your foot up in a vertical motion, shift your weight to your support leg, keeping it flexed. Bend forward slightly for balance.

You must bring your foot up to about knee high or better to provide a good striking surface. To make the inside of your foot even flatter, turn your ankle in an upward direction and scrunch up your toes. Ideally, the footbag should strike your foot on the side of the arch below the ankle.

Practice the Inside Kick without the footbag at first. With your hand, strike your foot in the approximate area where the footbag should make contact. Once you have the basic feel of this kick, you'll be ready to try it with the footbag.

The Inside Kick performed
correctly with the ankle
turned up.

When you practice with the footbag, toss it in the air so that it will fall directly in front of you and between your shoulders. Watch it during its fall, and time your kick accordingly. Your foot should meet the footbag at about knee level. Pop it up and catch it. If you're successful, practice with the footbag again and again until you have a smooth Inside Kick.

What's wrong? Instead of popping directly up in front of you, did the footbag fly off at a strange angle? If your Inside Kick makes the footbag suffer from such bizarre behavior, chances are that you're coming up too soon and making contact with the footbag too early. Slow down. Also, be sure to place your foot *under* the footbag and lift straight up, not out.

Another problem might be your form. Are you turning your ankle upward? If the contact point isn't as flat as possible, the footbag is bound to head off in an acute direction.

Once you have a fairly good grasp of the Inside Kick, you'll want to begin practicing the Outside Kick. It's all right that your Inside Kick isn't always as smooth as you'd like. By beginning the Outside Kick, you'll be able to inject some variety into your practice and to work at consecutive kicks.

OUTSIDE KICK

The Outside Kick is used when the footbag falls to the outside of either shoulder. If it drops on your right, you'll kick with your right foot. Similarly, if it comes down on your left, use your left foot.

*The Outside Kick
takes practice.*

Begin the Outside Kick by shifting your weight onto your flexed support leg. For balance, raise the hand on the same side above the shoulders.

With the balance arm up, lift the kicking leg to the side so that your foot is parallel to the playing surface. The lifting motion should be smooth, and you should strike the footbag at about knee level. The middle outside of the foot is used as a contact point. To help provide a flat striking surface, try pointing the toes up.

Visualize the Outside Kick and practice without a foot-bag at first. When you're ready to practice with the footbag, toss it in an arc designed to land approximately one step to your side.

Footbag is not a stationary sport. You must move your body to accomplish most of the kicks, and anticipating the footbag's flight path early will help you to maneuver into position. Once in position, take your stance and lean away from the footbag as you lift your foot. The body always leans away from the kick.

Many players make the mistake of allowing the body to come too close to the footbag's downward path. This con-fines the leg and causes the hips to rotate, putting the player in a cramped position.

To avoid this, step away from where the footbag is falling. This simple sideways motion will give you room to maneuver your foot into the correct position to provide a flat striking surface.

With an understanding of the Inside and Outside Kicks, you'll be able to string your kicks together into consecutives. Consecutives are kicks that keep the footbag airborne with-out drops in between. They come slowly at first. But with practice, you'll soon be kicking five, ten, and more consecu-tives.

And once you're stringing together consecutives, you'll want to learn more.

BACK KICK

If you want to have more range and control of the footbag, you'll want to learn the Back Kick. Though the most difficult of the three major kicks, the Back Kick will allow you to strike a footbag that has an end point behind the body with less effort.

Some players make the mistake of not learning the Back Kick. Instead, whenever a footbag passes overhead, they scramble backward to get into position for one of the other favored kicks. The Back Kick makes this awkward, backward maneuver unnecessary.

To begin the Back Kick, step forward into the path of the footbag as it approaches the upper body. Support your weight with the stepping leg. (There will be occasions when the footbag's path will end at a point *well* behind the player. If this is the case, step backward.)

Continue the Back Kick by rotating the arm and shoulder on the kicking side in the direction of the footbag's path. As you're maneuvering your upper body, raise the other arm to help balance the weight and bend the support leg. By twisting the upper body parallel to the footbag's flight, you'll allow it to pass while maintaining constant eye contact. The farther behind the body the footbag will fall, the more the upper torso has to rotate.

Don't kick until the footbag has passed the body. Then move your kicking leg in an arc that will put it directly beneath the footbag. Lift your foot straight up as you would with the Outisde Kick, making contact at about knee level or higher. Upon completion of the Back Kick, assume your ready stance.

The temptation with the Back Kick is to come up too early, hitting the footbag with the ankle or missing it entirely. But when performed with skill, it's a flashy kick and a good offensive weapon in footbag net.

The Back Kick is the most difficult kick to practice alone, so take turns with a friend at attempting this exacting move. Remember (1) to keep your kicking foot flat, (2) to bump the footbag rather than smash it, and (3) to use your raised arm as a counterbalance to help with the proper positioning of the kicking leg.

The two minor kicks are the Toe and Knee Kicks. Some players are likely to rely on these kicks too much, limiting their action. Neither of these kicks should be used unless absolutely necessary, and then they should be used, ideally, to set up an Inside or Outside Kick.

TOE KICK

Many beginning footbag players see the Toe Kick and think it will be the easiest to learn. Unfortunately, this isn't true. Because of the limited surface area for kicking, the Toe Kick is actually quite difficult for beginners to master.

The Toe Kick provides players with a quick reach to save a footbag when one of the other kicks won't do. The top part of the foot on the toes is used to flip the footbag back into play. But because of the limited striking area, there is little telling where the footbag will wind up.

Begin the Toe Kick by shifting your balance to the support leg. As the footbag falls to the ground, raise the kicking leg slightly and flex the knee, making contact low and close to

The Back Kick. Notice how Scott Hughes rotates the upper portion of his body toward the footbag.

It looks easy, but the Toe Kick is difficult.

The Knee Kick

the ground. Lean the upper body *away* from the kick. To assist with a flatter kicking area, curl the toes upward and use a flicking motion to give lift to the footbag. Almost like a wave, this motion should begin with the kicking leg, extend through the ankle, and end at the toe.

KNEE KICK

The Knee Kick is used primarily to prevent the footbag from striking the midsection of the body. Most players use it as a block to slow the footbag, setting up one of the more reliable kicks. Unfortunately, some players rely too much on the Knee Kick because of the large striking area and fail to develop their other kicking skills.

When the footbag is aimed directly toward you and its angle makes the Inside Kick awkward, use the Knee Kick. Almost like a high-stepping march, balance on the support leg while lifting the kicking leg until the thigh is parallel to the ground. Push the footbag upward by making contact just above the kneecap. Complete your play by using the Inside or Outside Kick.

CHAPTER FIVE

TIPS FOR SUCCESS

Nobody becomes expert at footbag overnight, though beginners *are* likely to master the Footbag Fetch. In the early stages, the footbag simply will not stay airborne. Accept this fact. But also accept the fact that with practice, you will get better.

There are steps you can take to reduce the number of drops you'll experience. But please note: I said *reduce,* not *eliminate.* Learning is part of the challenge of footbag.

Dedicated bodybuilders know that correct form is critical to achieving desired results. A person can lift weights incorrectly for years—and still look like Mr. or Ms. Average. On the other hand, a person can adhere to proper lifting and accomplish significant results in a relatively short period of time.

Footbag is no different. There is a *right* way to attempt each kick. That is why it is critical for you to have a mental grasp of each kick before you attempt it with the footbag. Bad habits are picked up easily, and they are difficult to break. Study each kick and perform it initially without the footbag. Only when you feel you understand the mechanics involved should you attempt a kick with the footbag.

Using the right stance is as important as form. The starting or waiting stance is identical to the basic athletic stance used in most sports. While waiting for your turn or while tracking the path of the footbag, stand with your feet pointing straight ahead, about shoulder-width apart. Your knees should be slightly bent, and your weight should be low and forward on the balls of your feet. This last point is important if you want to consistently place the footbag. To make sure that your weight remains low and forward, concentrate on keeping the support leg bent while kicking.

Equally important is the use of the arms and upper body as a counterbalance to get the kicking foot into correct position. With the Outside Kick, for example, there should be an imaginary straight line from the outstretched arm (the counterbalance) through the body to the kicking foot.

The kicking motion used in footbag is unique to footbag. In other kicking sports, players kick the ball away from the body. In footbag, a lifting motion is used to keep the footbag airborne. The lift is achieved by lifting the foot straight up, rather than away from the body.

For best results, kick the footbag slow and low (at about knee level). The kicking speed should be about the same as that of the footbag. Most beginning players play too fast. Think *bump,* instead of *smash!*

Few people are ambidextrous; that is, most people favor either their right or their left hand. The same is true of feet. Beginning footbag players tend to use one foot over the other. Advanced players, however, strive to use both feet equally. It's almost as if they divide their bodies in half with an imaginary vertical line. Each time the footbag falls on the left of that line, they take the kick with their left foot. When it falls on the right, they take the kick with their right foot. To reach this level of excellence requires intentional practice on your weak side.

Dutch Holland keeps the footbag airborne
by lifting his foot straight up.

With so many kicks, you might wonder how to determine in advance which kick to use. First, remember that there are only three major kicks: Inside, Outside, and Back. These kicks should be used most of the time. Use the Inside Kick if the footbag falls low directly in front of you and you can step into it. If the footbag has an end point to the side of the body or outside the width of the shoulders, use the Outside Kick. The Back Kick is reserved for passes directly above, overhead, or behind.

But how do you know if the footbag is going to fall in front, to the side, or behind? Concentration. As with all sports, concentration is the key to success. Every ounce of visual concentration must be focused on the footbag. If you don't concentrate, it will be difficult for your foot to connect with anything other than air.

Footbag is competitive. Then again, it's cooperative. A courtesy toss to another player always begins a rally. Similarly, players applaud each other with a "Good save" or "Nice play," and offer encouragement and suggestions with the goofs. Though courtesy isn't a skill that will help you kick better, it adds to the camaraderie. And it is one of the reasons that millions of players all over the world are kicking footbags.

CHAPTER SIX

FOOTBAG FREESTYLE

Nearly everyone who has played footbag experiences the excitement that comes when the concentration is focused and the footbag sails smoothly under control, kick after kick. But as with any sport, the initial excitement is apt to wane unless new challenges are introduced. Enter the world of footbag freestyle.

Freestyle is the artistic interpretation of footbag. It combines the sheer beauty of ballet with the mental concentration of the martial arts and the flowing energy of gymnastics, all choreographed to music. Outstanding freestylers are as precise as the best stage performers, and their appearance at any footbag tournament is a sure audience grabber.

Allowing the player to kick and play in any manner desired, freestyle is the only footbag sport that permits upper body contact. Simply, it is free-form play where anything goes. Anything? Well, anything that is graceful and smooth.

Footbag freestyle comes in two forms of play: individual and group. Individual freestyle puts the player center stage. Like a dancer, the soloist interprets music by carefully moving through a prearranged sequence of steps and kicks. Group freestyle offers two or more players the chance to coordinate precision moves through cooperative effort. In each, the winning point is rhythm.

Most freestyle kicks are basic kicks performed in an advanced, or trick, form. And the most important part of performing any freestyle move is the set-up kick. This allows the trick to come off smoothly, but requires skill and footbag control to do.

A flier probably will be the first freestyle move you'll learn. It is any basic kick (chapter four) performed in an airborne position. To perform any flier, set the kick and jump straight up. If you concentrate on *up,* rather than out, you'll be able to reset yourself or to complete a pass to another player.

The "wow!" moves are the clipper and the flying clipper. Both are attractive moves and are similar to the Inside Kick because contact with the footbag is made on the inside surface of the shoe. But they differ from the Inside Kick by crossing the kicking foot under the opposite leg.

To set the clipper, you want to place the footbag slightly in front and to the outside of your body. Step forward with your support foot, stepping just past the end point of the footbag's flight, and place your kicking foot in position behind your support leg. As with the other kicks, you want to lift straight up. For a flying clipper, jump straight up and take the kick in the air!

Another dramatic freestyle move is the delay, or stall, where the footbag is stopped in flight on the surface of the foot or on any part of the player's body. It is accomplished by moving the kicking foot in the downward motion of flight and

Fliers are show-stopping kicks performed in the air. They come in a variety of styles and difficulties.

Facing page: The clipper is similar to an Inside Kick, except it is taken behind the support leg. Above: The stall momentarily stops action.

at the exact speed of the footbag. This gives the kicker the chance to "stop action," while keeping the footbag elevated. Its simple appearance is deceiving because a stall takes perfect touch, ultimate timing, and practice. Drama at its very best!

Whether performing a basic kick or a flying clipper, freestyle moves are not made by happenstance. Hours of planning go into choreographing the kicks to a particular musical piece, with many freestylers noting on paper which kicks will work in each section of a song.

A big disappointment at some freestyle events is when kickers show up unprepared. A few kickers adopt a nonchalant attitude about the importance of planning to their routine and decide to freestyle to someone else's leftover music. They throw in a clipper here and a stall there. Their moves fail to flow from one kick to the next and, in general, their performances lack polish. Remember, freestyle has rhythm and precision. You can't freestyle well if you don't know what your next move is going to be.

And if you doubt the importance of music to performance, imagine a movie without the musical background. It's flat. All of the psychological play that music provides is missing.

Sometimes it's rock. Sometimes it's classical. But the music should always complement the kicks, and vice versa. To collect judges' points in freestyle, plan your music and your moves.

CHAPTER SEVEN

FOOTBAG SPORTS

Footbag is a good way to express yourself, and kickers enjoy the artistic statement that freestyle makes even when judges award higher points to someone else. But if your idea of sport involves tough competition—player against player, team against team—then perhaps one of the other footbag sports will appeal to you.

Once you leave the freestyle arena, fancy kicks are not a necessity, though skill with the basic kicks is a must, as play is restricted to the lower body. Players rely on Inside and Outside Kicks to place the footbag. Toe and Knee Kicks become important blocks to help set up the more desired kicks. And the Back Kick comes to the forefront as an aggressive tool.

What are the other footbag sports? Actually, there are several from which to choose, and each offers something different to the players.

FOOTBAG CIRCLE

Even though it is not an "official" footbag sport and isn't seen in WFA competition, the footbag circle is the most common form of play. Seen in schoolyards everywhere, the circle has no precise definition because the "rules" vary with the players and circumstances. Many players use the circle purely as a form of practice, with participants kick-passing the footbag to other players across the circle, practicing whatever kicks seem most appropriate. (A commonly followed rule is to use the Inside Kick if the footbag falls inside the circle and the Outside Kick if the footbag has an end point outside the circle.) But sometimes players don't kick *across* the circle. Instead, they kick the footbag from foot to foot to foot, keeping the footbag rotating in a continuous circle.

In other circles, the kickers practice consecutives before passing the footbag. Sometimes a maximum number of consecutives is set and when that number is reached, the kicker must pass the footbag to another player. At other times, a time limit is set. Still in other circles, a player kicks until the footbag is dropped. Then a courtesy toss is given to another player.

One interesting variation of footbag circle is reminiscent of dodge ball. In this form, players kick the footbag back and forth across the circle. Players who miss their kick and allow the footbag to drop are eliminated from the kicking circle. Obviously, the last person remaining "in the circle" wins.

Footbag circles vary in number from 2 to 25 or more, with the largest recorded circle having 862 players. All circles, however, share the same objective: Keep the footbag in the air.

FOOTBAG CONSECUTIVE

If you like competing with yourself, as well as with other people, and want the chance to break world records, then footbag consecutive is for you. The idea is simple: Keep the footbag in the air as long as possible.

If the idea is simple, the skill required to accomplish such a feat is not. Your Inside and Outside Kicks *must* be reliable or your consecutive kicks will never get off the ground. Many of those who participate in consecutives alternate the footbag between the left foot and right, and try to avoid the Toe and Knee Kicks because of their unreliability.

Footbag players use consecutives as a personal scoring system. Each kick is worth one point. Players often recount their successes to each other by reeling off their best consecutive score. The higher your score, the more footbag control you demonstrate.

In competition, there are singles divisions for men and women, and a doubles division complicates play by limiting each kicker to twenty-five consecutive kicks, at which point a pass must be made to the partner. A more difficult doubles "one pass" exists for players who want the ultimate challenge; partners must pass the footbag with *each* kick.

Average scores tend to pale next to the world record scores. Consider this: The world record for men's singles is 32,598 and for women's singles, 12,838. The doubles world record is 33,333.

How many consecutives can you kick?

FOOTBAG GOLF

If you're of the opinion that golf is a sport for people who aren't agile, try footbag golf and you'll change your mind. Though similar to standard or disc golf, footbag golf challenges the player to place the footbag into a designated area or "hole" by kicking.

The "hole" is usually a cylinder about 18 inches (45 cm) in diameter which is elevated 36 inches (90 cm) on a dowel. The footbag must be placed *in* the cylinder to count. Informally, players improvise by marking the "hole" with a flat cir-

cle about 8 inches (20 cm) in diameter cut from plywood or hardboard.

Players start by teeing off, or kicking the footbag in the direction of the green. The object is to get as close to the hole as possible and to stay out of the rough. It may sound easy, but the shots are seldom clear. The nine- or eighteen-hole courses are set up around "hazards"—sometimes a clump of bushes, or a cluster of trees, or even a duck pond. (Be careful with this one. A footbag won't float for long!)

Once each hole has been played and the total circuit completed, scores are tallied. The person with the fewest total strokes (kicks) is the winner.

FOOTBAG NET

The ultimate footbag game is footbag net. It's volleyball played with the feet!

It is played on a 20 foot by 44 foot (6 m x 14 m) court that is divided into four equal serving quadrants. A 5-foot- (2-m-) high net divides the two sides.

Using the same scoring and rule system as for volleyball, players attempt to set, spike, and score by using a footbag. This is where the Knee Kick will come in handy as a block and where the Back Kick will become a valuable offensive weapon. But there is a hitch: In singles net, players are allowed only three consecutive kicks per side. If a player takes more, a point is scored for the opposing side. In doubles net, five kicks per side are allowed, but no single player can take more than three consecutive kicks.

This footbag golfer putts into the hole for a birdie.

*A real challenge, footbag net is volleyball—
played with the feet!*

If that isn't tough enough, you can play ultra footbag net. In ultra net, the number of consecutives is cut. Two are okay for singles and three for doubles, but in doubles no individual player can take more than two consecutives. And to make things just a bit more challenging, only feet may be used. No knees!

Game, anyone?

CHAPTER EIGHT

COMPETITION

You can learn about footbag competitions from flyers distributed at sporting goods stores, from other kickers, and from reading *Footbag World.* It's only natural for footbag players to get together to compare skills.

Often these events are informal, a group of friends gathering for fun. But other times, the contests are official, with prizes, ribbons, and trophies. The 1986 WFA World Championships, which drew competitors from five countries, had a twelve thousand dollar purse to divide between winners. And the stakes are growing.

Whether competing at an official event or an informal one, footbag players try to perform smoothly and consistently. If your kicks are executed with smooth style and with a consistent manner, you have a better shot at the prizes, especially in footbag freestyle.

Because it is a unique and artistic form of kicking, freestyle (see chapter six) is judged differently than the other footbag sports, with competitors judging their freestyle peers. There are several factors that judges consider before awarding points. A freestyler's *execution* of kicks should be without hesitation or awkward movement. The *variety* and

difficulty of the kicks is also an important consideration. One final area that judges look at in freestyle is the *presentation*; that is, they consider how the music and kicks work together to create an enjoyable experience for the viewer.

Other official footbag sports (see chapter seven) are judged objectively. Points are accumulated when you score against your opponent, and high score wins (except in golf where low score wins).

If you are the type of person who likes to compete in individual sports, rather than team sports, footbag is a natural for you, as all footbag sports either are designed for singles play or have singles categories. On the other hand, if you prefer being part of a team, try freestyle, consecutives, or net.

Contestants compete worldwide in four basic playing groups: Juniors (normally under 16 years old), Beginner (players who have just started or are competing in a tournament for the first time), Intermediate (players who have previously placed in the "Beginner" category), and Advanced/Professional. There are divisions for men, for women, and for mixed competition.

As footbag catches on like wildfire, the number of juniors players is on the rise. In 1986, the largest ever juniors tournament was held in California; as they make their presence known, even more juniors tournaments will appear.

Official play is sanctioned by the World Footbag Association. This body develops the rules by which all play is governed. It also sponsors the World Championships (open to intermediate and advanced/professional players) each

A freestyle team competes by displaying rhythmic, mirror-image moves.

year and coordinates training camps for players to learn new skills.

By competing, you can learn new kicks and get pointers from better players on how to improve your skills. Footbag competition is a true test of eye/foot coordination.

CHAPTER NINE

ATHLETES AND FOOTBAG

*I*t used to be that athletes participated only in activities directly related to their sport. Weight lifters wouldn't be found anywhere except in the weight room, and football players saw no need to practice anything except their plays.

Today, coaches are more enlightened. It's not uncommon to find weight lifters being scheduled into the weight room and the aerobic room. Some weight lifters are finding that a light aerobic session provides an excellent warm-up and stretch for the lifting they'll do later. Others are alternating weight lifting days with aerobic days to give their heart the exercise it needs and doesn't usually get from straight weight training. Similarly, professional tennis players are finding that a weight training program is beneficial to their game. Even professional football players are stepping up to a dance bar to practice ballet moves in order to enhance their on-field performance.

What today's coaches know is that a varied physical routine helps develop total body control and synchronization. That is, they have found that the development of complimentary skills enhances sport-specific performances. And some physical education specialists believe that this rounded approach to athletics has a beneficial effect on learning in the classroom.

Speed, agility, and strength are crucial to all sports, and many game-winning efforts have depended on them. Because footbag games aid the development of quickness and the range of mobility, they are a benefit to all athletes no matter what the particular sport.

Regardless of the scope of an athletic program, footbag drills may be added to enhance players' general performance.

ONE PASS

In one pass, two or more players work together on the three major kicks to develop control, agility, balance, and kicking rhythm.

Facing each other, the players stand about four or five feet apart and attempt not only to keep the footbag airborne, but also to use just one kick at a time.

WALL DRILL

The wall drill is great for athletic timing and cardiovascular strength. It's designed to improve the Inside Kick, with occasional use of the Outside Kick.

Standing two to three feet in front of a wall, the player repeatedly kicks the footbag against the wall and keeps it airborne by alternating the feet.

MULTIPLE FOOTBAG DRILL

The multiple footbag drill is good for developing footwork, quickness, and concentration.

A thrower will gather as many footbags into one hand as possible and toss them toward the kicker. With each toss, the thrower calls the kick to be attempted by the kicker.

To work on quickness, advanced players can speed up the drill and toss the footbag to the side to force movement.

THE RAINBOW

The rainbow is a good drill to focus on cardiovascular strength, coordination, and concentration, as visual contact must be maintained on the footbag to complete this activity. It stresses the outside Kick.

The footbag is tossed so that an Outside Kick is set up. Then the player continues the play from left outside to right outside, arcing the footbag overhead.

Footbag games, though fun in and of themselves, are great for warm-up and cool-down. Their pace makes them an excellent aerobic exercise. They are outstanding as an off-season conditioner for athletes because they reinforce the five Cs of athletic endeavor: concentration, coordination, communication, commitment, and control. The importance of these traits to all sports is recognized by coaches everywhere.

CHAPTER TEN

ORGANIZATIONS

Since 1983, footbag sports have been represented by the World Footbag Association. This organization establishes the rules and regulations that govern all official footbag sports. Membership in the organization includes a subscription to *Footbag World* and discounts on many footbag items and events. They sponsor touring teams which are available to demonstrate and teach footbag skills at schools and to train professional athletes. They may be contacted at the address below.

World Footbag Association
1317 Washington Avenue, Suite 7
Golden, Colorado 80401

Interest in footbag is worldwide. Other organizations promote festivals and tournaments under the auspices of the WFA. These local addresses might be of interest.

Australian Footbag Federation
P.O. Box 68
Lismore Heights
New South Wales 2480
Australia

Canadian Sipa Sipa Distributor
R & C Sports
278 Lockwood Street
Winnipeg, Manitoba
Canada R3N 1S2

Danish Footbag Association
Markvej 44 or Gl Kogelandevej 655
2660 Br Strand
Denmark

East Coast Footbag Association
142 Morris Avenue
Long Branch, New Jersey 07740

English Hacky Sack Distributor
Markitrade LTD
81-85 Carnwath Road Fulham
London 5W6 3H2
England

Japan Footbag Association
Nissho Iwai Corporation
4-5, Akasaka 2-Chome
Minato-ku
Tokyo 107
Japan

Swedish Footbag Association
Ryttmastaregatan 7
252 53 Helsingborg
Sweden

FURTHER READING

Cassidy, John. *Footbag: An Instructional Handbook.* Golden, Colorado: The World Footbag Association, 1985.

_____. *The Hacky Sack Book.* Stanford, California: Klutz Press, 1982.

Footbag World. The World Footbag Association, 1317 Washington Avenue, Suite 7, Golden, Colorado 80401.

INDEX

796.33 Brimner, Larry Dane
B
      Footbagging

$1

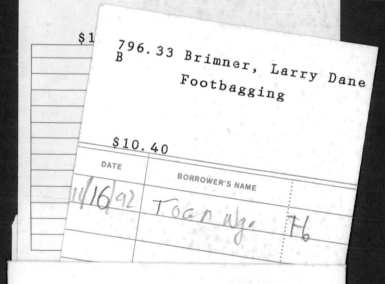

796.33 Brimner, Larry Dane
B
      Footbagging

$10.40

DATE	BORROWER'S NAME	
11/16/92	Toan uy.	76

© THE BAKER & TAYLOR CO.